Writer's Cramp

Spirita

Copyright © 2011 - TumbleBrush Press LLC

All rights reserved. No part of this publication may be reproduced, stored in a retrieval system, or transmitted in any form or by any means, electronic, mechanical, recording or otherwise, without the prior written permission of the publisher.

ISBN-13: 978-0615479743 (TumbleBrush Press)

Printed in the United States of America.

Published by TumbleBrush Press LLC
4860 Joliet St., Denver, CO, 80239
Buffalo, Wyoming
http://www.tumblebrushpress.com

Cover art by David Torres

Share your own Inspirations with us at:

Inspirations@tumblebrushpress.com

From SPIRITA, the voice in all of us speaking from our soul

Who is Spirita?

What is a Spirita?

Spirita is Twinkles.

Spirita is the Twinkle you see when you connect with someone.

Spirita is the Twinkle you feel when you get excited inside or gooey all over.

Spirita is the Twinkle you hear when a voice or music or nature communicates in special ways.

Spirita is not a person or a face or a shape or an object to see or hold.

Spirita is your Soul announcing your presence and welcoming inspirations.

Spirita is Awareness Transformed to Being.

Table of Contents

1	Relationships
2	Tormentus Relief
3	Diverted Daily Duties
4	A Sleepy Behavior
5	The Art of Translating
7	Rainbows for Marina - Treinta
9	Creative Illusion
10	A Robed Tome
12	My Computer's Friend
15	Daily Duties
16	Drudgery of being Sick
17	The Dirty Dish Connection
20	To Bed, or Not To Bed
21	Anguished Compositions
22	Medicinal Value
23	Time Value
24	Transcription
25	Solitude
26	Sharing
27	Causing
28	Wine
29	Dictionary
30	Seen But Not Heard
31	Unknown Sounds
32	Deranged Memory
33	Propagation
34	Reward
35	Convincing
36	Fixing Stuff
37	Flames
38	Night Exercises
39	Non-thinking
40	Insomnia
41	Technician
42	Obliterated Intentions

43	Compulsions
44	Creeping Inspiration
45	Bed
46	Computers
47	Regurgitation
48	Control
49	Revenue
50	Brit the Puppy
51	Creative Breathing
52	Performance
53	Clutching
54	Web
55	Provocation
56	Solace
58	Guiding
59	Context
60	Discovery
61	Heartbeats
62	Interrupting Inspiration
63	Done Expressing
64	Bed Light
65	Anonymity
67	Mary the Gifter
68	New Words
69	Favorite Pens
70	Writing Pens
72	Smart
73	Recycle Bin
74	Reasons For Writing
76	Anxiety
77	Bird Feeder
78	Copyright
79	Writing Paper
80	Cults
81	3 Hole Paper
82	Applaud Messages
83	Tracks
84	I've Got The Blues

85	Lonesome
86	Pen
87	Enough Is Not Enough
88	Rejection
89	Reverence
90	Skull Feathers
91	Words
92	Totem
93	Writing Space
94	Spring
95	Choosing
96	Grief
97	Gifting
98	Exercises
99	Colonists
100	AngelMagic
101	Emerging
102	Brooding Cliff
103	Discovery
104	Paperless
105	Writing In The Dark
106	Call of Creativity
107	Bored Writing Computer
108	Emotions Expressed
109	Guidance
110	Creative Experience
111	Diversion to Bed
112	Writing Demonstrated
115	Nairda's Dimensions - A Journey through the Twilight of Being
117	Nairda's Dimensions - One
120	Nairda's Dimensions - Two
127	Nairda's Dimensions - Footnotes
128	Extractions from Humanity - Introducing Cliff
130	Extractions from Humanity 1 - Dear Dad
131	Extractions from Humanity 2 - America (The Clydesdale)

132	Extractions from Humanity 3 - Dogmatically Stigmatized
134	Whispers -1 - From Cliff - About Wisdom
135	Extractions from Humanity 6 - Priceless Value
136	Extractions from Humanity 10 - Obama Ittis (Bushwhacked)
137	Extractions from Humanity 33 - True Manhood
138	Extractions from Humanity 34 - Acute Humility
139	Extractions from Humanity 24 - InFinite
140	Extractions from Humanity 65 - Question for the Vain
141	Honoring Cliff - Transmuting 4
142	Extractions from Humanity 121 A Very Wealthy Man
144	Extractions from Humanity 150 Trina
147	Honoring Spirit - Cliff I - 12
148	Extractions from Humanity 176 Trials And Tribulations
149	Writing By Cliff - The Liberty of Writing
151	Extractions from Humanity - A Collection of Observations
153	The American Dream - An Immigrant's Story
154	The American Dream One
156	The American Dream Two
159	The American Dream Footnotes
160	AngelMagic - Laura-Arual
162	Every Precious Moment One
164	Every Precious Moment Two
168	Every Precious Moment Three
170	Every Precious Moment Four
172	Every Precious Moment Footnotes
173	AngelMagic - Diary of an Angel
176	AngelMagic - Healing Hands
185	AngelMagic - AngelNotes

Writer's Cramp

Relationships

Writing can become

a friend and lover

in the absence

of another.

Tormentus Relief

When tormented with anxieties contrived from experiences created,
Writing is Relief.

When the compression of relationships contort energy,
Writing is Therapy.

When awaked at early times ante meridian from clogged brain wrenched,
Writing is Balm.

The flashing prompt on computer patiently waits while cogitating, but when it becomes annoying, write with a pen on paper because pen doesn't keep pulsating.

Writing becomes a friend, lover, therapist, confidant, angel, foil and funnel.
It never disappoints and constantly decompresses.

Discover the serenity writing shares every time you employ its magic.

Be equally impressed that its companionship is not offended when you fart.

Writer's Cramp

Diverted Daily Duties

Daily duties are often diverted

by a word in Soul

that explodes

into an exposition of writing

that amazes.

Writer's Cramp

A Sleepy Behavior

Write to sleep.

Sleep to have energy to experience.

Experience what you write.

Write what you experience.

Maybe this is just circular transference.

Maybe we are just full of crap.

That probably qualifies one as a writer.

The Art of Translating

Writing is viewed, by many adherents, as a skill learned through education and practice.

To others, writing is a grand talent naturally gifted and honed by gusts of inspiration.

To many, writing is gut-wrenching struggles to express a concept or feeling that continually eludes disclosure because the effort never mirrors the intent.

As with most definitions, writing includes all of these conditions.

Writing is the Art of Translating.

Although we may be schooled, inspired and can admit to struggles about writing, compositions are never our own creation.

It is not that we plagiarize, transform the ideas of others, or mimic a style not unique to ourselves, rather, we merely allow ourselves to translate from a litany of composition floating in the cosmos awaiting a font to express.

Like other translators, we will be given credit for the words we espouse.

Like other translators, we will be connected as the author of our stimuli.

Like other translators, we will appreciate the reception of our translations as if the words were unique to us.

But, admit to being merely a translator and the vessel and vassal for Soul.

You see - - we are endowed with sensitivity to Awareness.
Honor those around us by Awareness.
Honor inspiration by Awareness.
Honor the Energy-Of-All-That-Surrounds-Us by Awareness.
Honor desires and seeking and dreams and aspirations by Awareness.

Honor God by Awareness.

Through Awareness, translate what is heard and absorbed and felt.

It is an Art of Translating and Writing is the bounty.

Rainbows for Marina
Treinta

Enchanted by the never ceasing snowfall and comforted by the miracle asleep in my bed, I sit before this patient computer playing with words inspired by Soul.

> I admit to being a translator
> rather than a composer.

The sentences and phrases and goofy words I create emanate from a source celestial.

I cannot claim authorship because I do not feel ownership over these creations.

I accept responsibility for my blurbs and words and balderdash, while admitting that their genesis is beyond my persona.

I am reverent about Awareness I possess that allows me to translate perceptions into prose, but I am equally humbled by the reality that I am merely a messenger.

> The creature in my bed is a true author.
> Her prose is compassion and her
> method is unconditional love.

She composes bubbles with her energy that envelop the people around her and enchant them with her passion.

Marina writes with her spirit and composes on her dedication to the current object of her attention.

All of us are authors and messengers and translators of a divinity we share.

Marina and I define our own mission with the tools we adopt that reflect our choices of communication. Mine are more mundane. Hers are angelic.

As the snow continues to unconditionally caress the dominion outside my window, I honor the sleeping miracle in the next room with this tome to the bond we share.

Writer's Cramp

Creative Illusion

Nothing is transformed,

Rather,

It is illuminated.

A Robed Tome

There must be a natural stroke of the cosmic
clock at 3:00 a.m. that entreats Sleep to
enchant words rather than snores.

If it weren't so, I wouldn't be sitting in front of
my computer translating inspiration into marks
on paper.

Perhaps, though, it is really the Goddess of
Sleep
conspiring with Robe that hung unexercised
behind the bathroom door
until I donned it on this chilly winter night
while noise-monster Furnace forces itself
on the atmosphere inside Sanctuary.

This dilemma of cause need not be solved

because

the effect is I am here emoting.

And, as I attempt to circumscribe this plot,

I am content to allow the
energy from other sources

Writer's Cramp

to play with Soul

and describe the exercise.

My Computer's Friend

When my computer decided it wanted to visit its buddies at the store where it was purchased, it conspired to cause me to take it there by sending some smoke signals of distress.

>The computer guy said my "mother board had fried".

Being disdainful of all things technological, I allowed the computer aficionados to guide me to the solution for my unresponsive computer.

Their determination translated to my spending a bunch of money while they said things that were a foreign language to me.

>"These cures take time," they said.

My imagination conjured their elapsed time as justification for the overrated amounts of money they wanted just to push a few buttons and remove all the new stuff I bought from the boxes.

Anyway, while all this "takes time" transpired, I rediscovered the joys and comfort and inspirations from reading.

I bought some new books and dusted off some old ones I possessed and my world was enriched by the love offered to me from the words and eternal consciousness translated by other gifters.

Obviously, after a couple of weeks, the words on these pages reveal the presence of a friend for my old computer now residing on a shelf in my domain of weaving translations.

Although 'computer acquisition' is a common exercise, for me, it was a dramatic excursion to satisfy the longings of my technological buddy to have a kin sharing the space of our creative illustrations.

These 'common exercises' may be ordinary for most people, but I have determined to allow the world of technology to communicate with a new generation while I hone my skills on more simplistic expressions of energy. In other words, I have deliberately decided to avoid being a computer person.

I am grateful to be writing these translations of inspiration again. I am blessed to refresh the bounty from reading.

Writer's Cramp

I am equally determined to allow the technology world to pass me while I dedicate the energy it would consume to tickling your Soul with Sprouts of Love.

Writer's Cramp

Daily Duties

Mundane musings are often

                diverted by a word

    traveling in space

        that explodes

into an exposition

           of writing

                  that is
amazing

    because

translators are credited with communications
        merely observed.

Writer's Cramp

Drudgery of Being Sick

The drudgery of being sick

is mollified

because

it offers time

to write.

The Dirty Dish Connection

Later I will wash the dirty dishes that have accumulated while I write with this computer.

The dirty dishes are testimony to the nourishment I require for pursuing prose inspired by excuses to write rather than accomplish some other effort (like washing dishes) that may be more honorable. Writers need nourishment, you know, to sustain the proliferation of words translated from ethereal inspiration.

While struggling with my avoidance of the unwashed dishes, it occurred to me that writing about life issues reflects the exercise of contending with dishes, so, I have composed the following preambles to express those comparisons.

Murky Habits

For instance, when you wash dishes in the dark, you don't always dislodge all the residue. Likewise, as we waddle our way through the murkiness of life's habits, unless we dislodge our opportunities for experience, we will miss some dandy chances for enlightenment.

Procrastinations
It also occurred to me that allowing the dirty dishes to pile up unattended is a habitual procrastination similar to tossing in bed rather than writing these inspirations.

Appeasing
I don't know if my writing appeals to or appeases any celestial audience, but I sometimes leave a spoon in the sink so the dirty dish gods have something to play with.

Procrastination Tormentus
When the dirty dishes torment my sense of duty sufficiently, I whisk them clean as I perfunctorily perform that function without guilt while admitting to the reality that my preference is to procrastinate as I have successfully done with my novel for twenty-eight years, three months, fourteen days and accumulating hours.

Disability
I have a plate I use often because if is on the top of the stack and I have semi-tremulous fears that I might offend it into disability from over-use as I did my previous composing computer.

Opportunity
As I sit here struggling with the form and content of these platitudes, the opportunity to attend to the dishes becomes more of an attraction.

Fulfillment
Perhaps I will discover life-fulfillment when I contend with the reality that struggling with dirty dishes and writing represents the base behavior of my chosen condition.

To Bed, or Not To Bed

Although Soul is inspired

and chooses to invigorate prose;

in conflict,

Body prefers

to subordinate inspiration

to Bed.

Guess which wins.

Writer's Cramp

Anguished Compositions

Nights of earthly anguish

torment consciousness into concussions

bleeding fears and figments

tempered only by concessions to

composing confessions ethereal.

Writer's Cramp

Medicinal Value

The release experienced

by writing

seduces sleep.

It is a relaxant

unparallel

by medicine.

Writer's Cramp

Time Value

While writing,

time has no value

except when you switch

from the light in the ceiling

to the one

filling the window.

Transcription

Avoid taking credit

for inspirations

transcribing Soulbeats

of

sensations

immortal.

Solitude

Solitude invents anguish

eclipsed by the

ascension of awareness that

writing transcends

loneliness.

Sharing

Were I to share 'things' with you in the same manner you share 'things' with me,

it would be a task

duplicating.

So,

I choose to share with you and honor you with my own sense of creativity –

writing.

Causing

Writing gives cause to two conditions:

Illumination

and

Examination.

The second condition requires the first.

Writer's Cramp

Wine

We are not quite as clever

writing,

before

a

glass

of

wine.

Writer's Cramp

Dictionary

Quest to communicate

is

punctuated by dictionaries.

Writer's Cramp

Seen But Not Heard

The sobriety of writing is:

the audience

does not always

hear the words

they see.

Writer's Cramp

Unknown Sounds

The magic of writing is:

the audience

hears words

the author

does not see.

Deranged Memory

I always imagine I will recall

the trinkets of inspiration

caressing my imagination

until I try to extract them

from memory

deranged by sleep.

Writer's Cramp

Propagation

When Wit wilts;

go to bed.

Prone

seems to propagate

Pen.

Reward

Sometimes reward from writing

is to go back to bed

where you can

cling to a space

in the universe that

appreciates

Creative Energy.

Writer's Cramp

Convincing

Avoid trying to convince with writing.

That is the job of Soul.

Merely splatter words that jump out of fingers

because you can't sleep

or when

God gets bored

and

wants to play.

Writer's Cramp

Fixing Stuff

Sometimes writing computer

gets so cantankerous,

you have to go to bed

to fix it.

Writer's Cramp

Flames

Writing about

the dimensions of reality

can char serenity

until the ember of disclosure

ignites words

waiting to be heard.

Writer's Cramp

Night Exercises

When I write by pen and paper

at night in bed,

I exercise

when my right arm activates,

and then extinguishes

the light by my bed.

When I am exhausted

by this workout,

I just leave the light on.

Writer's Cramp

Non-thinking

You may seem

to expose prose

more efficiently at night

when literary urges

do not compete

with thinking.

Insomnia

After awakening,

it is delicious to discover

Bedside Table caresses

Inspirations

triggered by Insomnia,

memorialized by Pen

which found

an unoccupied place

on Writing Paper.

Writer's Cramp

Technician

Choose a certain Incarnation
that reflects Eternal Desire
experiencing Self
being You.

Choose to be an observer
and communicator.

Some would say this is a description of a
teacher.

But, by normal definition a teacher is credited
with some knowledge
they attempt to transfer.

Without espousing special knowledge;
rather choose to observe and
serve to reflect what is discovered.

That performance requires no knowledge –
only technique.

So, it appears this describes a technician
plying Craft
to be a mirror of 'what is'
using words to reflect.

Writer's Cramp

Obliterated Intentions

Sometimes,

it's possible

to get

too cute

with Computer

and obliterate

intentions.

Compulsions

Compulsions

greater than

the sum of

training and culture

inspire Messages

requiring

Translation.

Writer's Cramp

Creeping Inspiration

When literary inspirations

creep too quickly

into Consciousness

while prone with Bed,

just move

Pen and Paper closer

and allow Computer

time to rest.

Writer's Cramp

Bed

When Inspiration wearies,

Bed beckons.

Writer's Cramp

Computers

One

of the two things

to be appreciated

about writing with computers

is

they usually do

what they are told to do

without

objecting.

Writer's Cramp

Regurgitation

Writing

causes

Soul

to

regurgitate.

Control

Computer has captured such

control over actions,

we often cease writing

just because

Printer

is out of paper.

Revenue

If ability

to generate revenue from writing

matched the verbosity

of prose,

Pocketbook

wouldn't be

so empty.

Brit the Puppy

Brit-Puppy moans and groans a lot

from her sleeping pad beside my
bed when I awake to

compose nocturnal inspirations.

At first I thought she was impressed

by my bursts of creativity.

Finally, I determined she is mostly irritated

by the sudden light

from the bedside lamp.

Creative Breathing

Being creative

is as fundamental

to happiness

as air

is to

breathing.

Performance

If we performed

with as much understanding

as expressed in our writing,

we would be constant

Inspiration.

Writer's Cramp

Clutching

When other actions

confound creativity,

clutching Bed

seems to

prompt prose.

Web

Sense writing

as

a web

waiting

for

a spider.

Writer's Cramp

Provocation

As with any provocative literature,

these translations

may perturb or please you.

Isn't it grand

that YOU will create

the effects of that choice?

Solace

A blanket wired with electrical currents

provides solace for body parts

exposed to an atmosphere

where writing occurs

while facing Computer

that doesn't care

if Room Temperature

Is

60 degrees Fahrenheit.

In that situation,

a wired Blankey

tempts termination

Writer's Cramp

of Inspiration

pulsating in competition

with atmosphere.

Guiding

We who have listened

To Heartbeats

from Soul,

have a responsibility

to translate

and transfer the messages sensed.

We are a gift

to guide,

but, not to teach;

for teaching often only

transfers knowledge

while disregarding Awareness.

Writer's Cramp

Context

Reviewing translations

to ensure

context

can successfully

chart a

path to

Bed

when responsibility

is secondary

to slumber.

Discovery

Discover

creativity

by writing;

to

re-energize

Body

and

reconnect

with Soul.
Writing

Writer's Cramp

Heartbeats

H – E – A – R - T – B – E – A – T - S

These translations

are like Heartbeats;

each one

enriches

your opportunity

for Inspiration

to create

your own Messages and Massages.

Writer's Cramp

Interrupting Inspiration

Sometimes, Inspiration

pauses

when you

are out of paper

to write on.

Writer's Cramp

Done Expressing

Sometimes,

you know you're done

expressing

when you

get to the

bottom of

the page

and don't

have any space left.

Writer's Cramp

Bed Light

During night,

Bed Light

promotes Inspiration

so It can get

some exercise.

Anonymity

Personifying

writing

dilutes

the

message.

Historically and habitually, written words are attributed to someone as 'Author'. When the mask of 'originality' is removed, all words flow from Divine Inspiration rather than mortal perspiration.

We are merely translators of energy vibrating to expression.

The genesis of written words is Spiritual Communal.

Writer's Cramp

Expressions through writing are gifted by Awareness.

In reality, attribution for written expressions should be "Anonymous".

Mary the Gifter

Words

--weaving in, out

about our being—

lending lyrics

to the melodies

of our life---

hopes----

dreams.

                        Mary   11/06

Mary the Gifter weaves joy by her Awareness of other's dimensions. She gifts books cradling Spirit that meshes into hallow creases seeking hope. She gifts food laced with Love that nourishes the belly, senses and Soul. Her penchant to morosely dwell depletes her Energy and diverts her Gifts. Realigned, Mary becomes Weaver creating Ripples blessing her Web.

Writer's Cramp

New Words

Decide to discover some new words.

The ones we use so much kinda' lose their allure.

Maybe we need to find some more words like Skookum.
They say Skookum is Canadian for 'strong'.

It really doesn't matter if that's true.
Skookum sounds different and just slides along over the teeth and tongue to create a sound that's unique.

If Skookum really does mean what they say it means,
that's even better.

A good meaning makes a good word special.

So what do you think is a Zu Zu Jug, or Goomee?

Writer's Cramp

Favorite Pens

Favorite pens

are the ones that always

write stuff you like

and don't make blobbly marks

even when they are cantankerous.

Writing Pens

My writing pens
are kinda' like money.

Sometimes I have too many.

Sometimes I cannot find them.

They show up when I don't need them.

When I'm desperate for one, they are elusive.

I tried to have so many, I would never be without.
But, I discovered there is no such thing as 'too many'.

Everyone else seems to have all they need.
I just hum along without a clue about how to keep mine.

Maybe I can convince someone that writing pens are like money
and sell a few to those seeking riches.

Writer's Cramp

Maybe I will just keep one trusty pen
companion
and use it to write these verses.

If you buy some of these poesies of prose,
then, my writing pen is like money.

I kinda' like that idea.

Smart

When we are

as smart

as Computer Printer,

we will

possess extra toner

for the 'thing'

so it doesn't

leave streaks on pages

of prose

at 2:00 a. m.

when we are attempting

to impress some 'sweet thing'

with words seeking to display.

Writer's Cramp

Recycle Bin

When there is

more paper

in the recycle bin

by Writing Computer

than in the three-ring binder

your writings fill,

you are probably

paying attention

to your Inspirations.

Reasons For Writing

Folks write

for three different reasons:

1. To make $$.
(most do not)

2. To express something to sway.
(mostly nobody is listening)

3. To cleanse their Soul for more Inspiration.
(This is kinda' like taking a crap)

My Buddy Cliff writes because he can't sing too good.

The pertinent answer to the question, "Why do people write?" can be discovered
when we become Aware that existence was created for two Opportunities:

To Experience

To be Creative.

Writer's Cramp

Experience allows us to know Relativity which
is the path to
Declare Who We Choose To Be.

Being Creative is the path to
Demonstrate our Partnership with God.

Writing chants Experience while proclaiming
Creativity.

Since Cliff can't profoundly express his
Creativity by singing, he writes.

Anxiety

When Anxiety

draws near

and pierces every cell

with floundering and festering;

writing with computer or pen

dismisses the clamor

of desperation

quelling disturbing habit

to calm

until comfort

is embraced

from words

propelling Spirit.

Bird Feeder

Write

as if you were a bird feeder:

invite all who choose

to imbibe;

provide fuel

for Spirit;

encourage those sharing

to cast a few aware-shells

for others to enjoy;

tease participants

with entry orbs

large enough to distribute enjoyment

while challenging inclusion.

Copyright

Why

do unpublished people

worry about their "copyright"

when propelling their words

could soothe and inspire?

It's as if they want to protect

their poop

in case someone

offers to make fertilizer from it.

Writing Paper

If you forget

writing paper

when you journey

from Sanctuary,

Inspirations

may need a place to inscribe.

Washing pen marks

from the palm of your hand

is not usually a sign

of organization.

Cults

Promoting 'authors'
of written material
is akin to promulgating
a culture of Cults.

Rather than
embracing, honoring and cherishing
Messages inspired
THROUGH these 'authors',
we dissect their genealogy,
preen their personality,
glorify their idiosyncrasies,
and market their 'charm'
as if they deserve
Cultish Certification.

Their words recede
as Personality is Embellished.

What does this charade declare for our
Values?

3 Hole Paper

To give 3-Hole-Paper-Puncher

some rest,

purchase

3-Hole-Paper.

Applaud Messages

When we cease nominating

authors for platitudes

and instead applaud

message of spirit,

the process of translating inspiration

will inhale meaning

and exhale honoring.

Writer's Cramp

Tracks

While writing,

be like a deer.

Leave tracks

of Awareness

without disturbing

the natural beauty

of your surroundings.

I've Got The Blues

"I've got the Blues"

sayeth

the poet

searching for

identity and charity

of Spirit.

"Here is a pen!"

offers friend

who comprehends

the dimensions experienced

sharing solution immortal

and memorable.

Writer's Cramp

Lonesome

LONESOME

can afflict

even when Body is amongst

acquaintances.

When LONESOME

diminishes,

seek solace

from writing.

Words birthed

are friends forever.

Pen

Always carry

a writing pen

and paper.

You never know when

the Twinkle Fairies

will splotch

your Awareness.

Inspiration disappears

when not quickly captured.

Writer's Cramp

Enough Is Not Enough

When you think

you have enough

words and pages

to publish

a tome,

and then

you discover

an error in math;

you gotta'

create more stuff

to fill in the voids.

Rejection

Rejection
stems energy flow
to reservoirs
disrupting comfort and health.

Writing,
to share observations
of conditions common to all Souls
encourages energy to discover
paths connecting Spirit.

Discoveries propelled
from these Spiritual connections
dissolve obstruction
of energy flow
until natural warmth
accompanies comfort
restoring health.

Reverence

Revering

a tome

comprising hundreds of pages

brings perspective

to the dedication

writers pledge

when initiating

Inspiration

translated to writing.

Skull Feathers

Feathers displaying skulls

peeking from outlines defining,

are merely

interpretation.

Likewise,

Reader embracing words

while discovering messages

unintended by author,

discovers skulls

everywhere.

Writer's Cramp

Words

Words

do not achieve notoriety

through multiplicity.

Words charm when

enchanted and charted

with economy

and simplicity.

Totem

Discover
a Totem
to guard your
written Inspirations.

Turtles
might be a choice
to grace writing computer
or surface holding paper and pen.

Perhaps you will choose
a depiction of Angels,
or parrots, or dolphins,
or elephants, or porpoise,
or a picture of a cherished one.

Totems offer us comfort
while they inspire,
mentor, partner
and share their energy.

Writing Space

A room or space

especially for writing;

adorned with tools, ornaments,

remnants, results and relishes

of writing;

offers transcendence

for Spirit

while providing

Sanctuary

for

Awareness.

Spring

When Spring

springs an Equinox to delight

our ennui with Winter,

the occasion

offers Opportunity

to celebrate with words

sprouting shoots

of Awareness

promising to be Blossoms

enchanting

as collections

of verse and prose

delighting our senses.

Choosing

Writing

is Opportunity

to declare

Who We Choose To Be,

and then,

describe a path

delineating

How Do We Get There.

Opportunity

awaits Awareness

declaring

Inspiration.

Grief

Grief is a heavy dimension
absorbing energy
and diverting attention
until Mind, Body and Emotions
are soggy and chilled
denying Joy and Peace.

Antidotes to Grief
are elusive and fleeting
while dismay plagues senses.

Writing,
to release reaction
and express energy diminished,
cannot replace Hollowness,
but,
as expression progresses during writing,
balance returns to Spirit
and,
words honoring,
replenish dented relativity.

Gifting

Were I
to gift to you
my Soul,
and that would
encourage you to write,
I would do it instantaneously.

Were I
to hand to you
my Heart
and that would
inspire you to enchant words to paper,
I would share reverently.

Were I
to transfer
the Energy of Spirit
and that would
transform reluctance to express,
I would connect to you eternally.

Who I Am
is yours
as unconditional Gift
to Create Awareness
that you
are Gifted.

Exercises

There are many exercises
that expose and express
our Creativity.

Writing is profound illumination for Soul
and effective therapy
for dented Spirit.

For those of us financially compromised,
writing is budget conscious
since it only requires pen and paper.

As balm for morose dimensions,
as fuel for exhausted propulsions,
as salve for bruised connections,
as energy for diminished sensations,
Writing
is an exercise
limbering our Spirit,
stretching our Imagination,
powering our Inspiration,
and
providing Peace
to our Desperations.

Writer's Cramp

Colonists

When Writers
see themselves
as Messengers gifted to translate,
rather than,
a Colony of Consequentialists
to be revered,

then,

Message
will become more important
than persona
presenting it

and Value

will be restored to this Gift.

Writer's Cramp

AngelMagic

Write

as if you have

an Angel on your shoulder

whispering

in your ear

while tickling

your fingers

with

AngelMagic.

Writer's Cramp

Emerging

There is little experience

in life,

that compares

to witnessing

Emergence of Creativity

by Spirits

compressed

with doubts

about their Inspirations.

Writer's Cramp

Brooding Cliff

Cliff, who authored

"Extractions From Humanity"

broods and breeds

Words

by copulating with

his Soul

to Divine

discovery, dismay, disgust

and determination

for the anguish, assaults and awareness

that humanity

possesses and lacks.

Discovery

Discover

creativity

by writing;

to

re-energize

Body

and

reconnect

with

Soul.

Paperless

While writing

in the middle of the night,

and Computer Printer

runs out of paper and

you have no reserve of sheets,

sometimes, you just have

to go to Bed

to recover.

Writer's Cramp

Writing In The Dark

Writing in the dark

is kinda' exciting

because, later,

you really don't know

what you said

until

you turn on the light.

Call of Creativity

The Call of Creativity

manifests in many ways.

For those of us blessed with inspiration

to translate words caressing our Soul,

we often write to keep our sanity.

It is the only form of expression

where we are guaranteed

someone will listen,

because we have to read our own stuff

to see if what we write

is cute and clever.

Writer's Cramp

Bored Writing Computer

When Writing Computer gets bored,

it sends Twinkle Fairies

to tickle Imagination

and fan Fascination

until Bed jiggles

to Silliness

causing

Body to arise

in Response.

Emotions Expressed

Writing

is not an Art:

Writing is emotions

expressed;

lingering to be

consumed cautiously,

or tumbled curiously

or enjoyed passionately

until ennui or Awareness prevail.

Writer's Cramp

Guidance

The Spirit

of Awareness

will guide Soul

to Inspiration and Creativity,

which is how Writers express.

Creative Experience

When we finally accept

our purposes as humans

are simply to Experience

and Create,

the Desperation we Imagine

to Dramatize our Silliness

fades to the

Joy of Discovery.

Writer's Cramp

Diversion to Bed

When Sweetie only grunts

at my bedtime humor

or moans at my interpretation

of sensuality,

I exit Bed

and Bubble myself

composing at writing computer

with Inspirations Twinkling Spirit

and satiating Soul until

I blissfully smother Bed with

attention and gratefully

swirl "I Love You" to the Angel

Blessing Blankey with her Presence.

Writer's Cramp

Writing Demonstrated

Snatches of Writing
From UnProclaimed Spirits

Writing is not an art requiring special training.

Writing is not a science promoted by
education and rules of composition.

Writing is Awareness Expressed.

Writing reveals emotions and
spirit and observations
in natural flow comfortable to
the translator of Messages.

We have designated translators of Awareness to be 'authors' while all who are so termed will admit to revelations that transcend their natural abilities. Thus, they are merely transmitting Inspirations which chose these Spirits as Messenger.

Kindly treat yourself to the following Snatches offered by UnProclaimed Messengers.

Discover your own Awareness.

Propel your words to paper and Bless with Inspiration.

Whether publicized or privately enjoyed,
allow Writing to become
a friend and companion
always available when Serenity beckons.

Nairda's Dimensions

A Journey through the Twilight of Being

A climate of logical progression, apostrophes in the right places, structured families, chorded music, linear communication, concise concepts, and singular focus are relativities foreign to some spirits captured by altered reality.

Nairda is one of those Souls.

Cause is not as relative as reality for Nairda, because cause only diverts us from embracing the vibrations guiding and emanating from Nairda's Dimensions.

To most of us, Nairda's Dimensions are complex and confusing because Nairda revolves around impulses and values we do not easily assimilate. Consequently, we often react with frustration and sometimes anger about Nairda's behavior. But, this merely reflects our inability to comprehend how Nairda filters vibrations and information and then translates these impulses into presentations.

For Souls reflecting Nairda's dimensions,

many common values and reactions
can be deeply confusing and confronting.

Kindly embrace the expressions of Nairda's
Dimensions
composed by Adrian.

Nairda's Dimensions

One

Growing up my life I feel like I was always alone on the way home from school, even sometimes at home.

I can't believe that even sometimes now I can't remember being a kid. Maybe their was little things that I can remember like my Communion, 1-5 grade, special concerts or something, or the little boy and girl kisses in the back of the school.

The moving around a lot because of separations, drugs, family, and things that just hurt people. I have already 25 years have been through a lot of tribulations, and it seems like every time I am close to thinking of life in my mind that I must have an angel watching me or "god" as I said Dear Lord Jesus is about to make something special happen either because I feel it should be done or it's the right thing in my mind. These situations don't go away and I can't explain but I try. I guess I' am hoping this is not what a mid life crisis is, because I think I 'am just young trying to enjoy life.

Experience has everything to do with life and the value that we respect. I have treated people with respect and still feel abominated about how life really is. I feel every body has their owned up to opinion and, or has felt like they were disrespected changing lifestyles, childhood, sex, family, and every body owns up to their opinion. I feel right now in life that life is somehow saying respectively you know what are you supposed to be doing and what you have expected your lives accounts to be and then thinking the vast majority which is most likely ahead of you is like a majority rule kinda situation that just gives you the "kinks". Like if I was "kinky".

The whole ideal is that someone is not going to pay your way through life you have to make your way through on your own, it just takes time. Trust and friendship also works, keeping exposure and motivation also moves the body also helps as where more of natural ability also counts. Everybody helps along the way by showing way of mobility, and that creates pressure that helps bond of friendship, a friendship can go along way.

Being yourself helps escape the pressures in life and definitely will boost your confidence.

I like school because Education is really the number one choice in my life, besides work, and my little girl. I find that a career is most of my concern, and part of this diversity or schedule of friends, family, co-workers, and then managing I believe is what leads to success.

Personally devotion is what I' am sure I will hear for along time not always knowingly what I might do next, BUT THAT MIGHT BE incorrect because honesty will probably take its toll while not thinking to yourself ahead of time. If this is correct I would only hope that it is, well the truth I know, but the only thing I can feel I do not know everything.

Nairda's Dimensions

Two

Writing and a good day can have a lot in common, taking both leadership and partnership. Partnership comes from the encountering of one another based on living everything. Leadership comes from the understanding that one person is trying to bring forth.

Life weighs down a lot and can grow on a person. Full of life's creativity, person and comfort can make the situation acceptable. Situations mature on humility and the growth and how humility makes itself found.

Lifelike and being lifelike takes its tolls as we start to progress in growing up. Simply, life and many of its roads are capable of being followed. I 'am only a student and as far as I know steps of achieving can be only doing right things and changing misconceptions.
Most of what I have been dealing with.

I 'am also a person with a daughter that is four years old, four years ago she was born. I don't know exactly what a young life is or feels like from her perspective.

I remember being pushed to learn, and then I guess not much friends and then parents that split up. I also remember that my family was really close to wanting to be part of a religion, and then was the era I would call something like the entrepreneurs of wise cracks.

My daughter, I felt excited that day, but at the same time I never knew really what was going to be the first step, but I knew that quitting was not a reason to go and do it. That would have had to have been one of life's greatest moments. "Wow" she was born! Only so small though, but the room was felt. Disappointing enough I knew from here on out either "you were there", or just part of the paper signing. Still am glad to have had one that I can call mine, "Hey! By the way she was mine". More or less I was going to have a friendship that I was sure I can count on. Frowning, crying, babying, and oh the "views" "smells" "detecting" well how about you?

Well, life I was average I guess I would say. and "very well put I would say." Not occurring to me every calculated step, but expecting the best of every outcome "I sure hope I wasn't the only one". Sports and family, family and friends always was a good place to be, sometimes elsewhere was a better place to be.

How about the times when occasions were big like prom and you're expecting everything, your suit and friends, ride, and then your name wasn't called but still made the dance big. Or at the end of the night you find out your date was regret made by friends, and I know she was very cool, always around.

For a few years I was always moving around looking for jobs because I felt being uncomfortable had been there, but for me there was always somebody or something to help get by. Struggling and I had been getting along pretty well, but the task had always been at hand.

Whether it was sports, family, friends, and struggling Adrian was growing up. It's hard growing up especially if things you manage to do aren't so great. Adrian had an attitude that needed a big change at least I thought I was doing so. "Yeah, I was working hard." My view is probably brief but I feel as a person that I 'am doing only what I can to try, to try and deserve more.

Being Hispanic really just made my person want to achieve more. I have heard a lot that myself I wasn't going to make it in life any where, and from people themselves knowing that they might not make their place somewhere I the world, and it only takes a little for me to want to do more and complete.

I feel as if I should want to complete what needs to be done, but had to be said "again I'm not perfect, I may need a pushing." Alright so what, I think this may not be the best educated conversated meaning of understanding of a perfect life because I'm far from it. I totally understand the "yes" I should have pushed harder, farther I mean without some of the lying I did. Lying relates to money, friends, education, and I feel that everything that is, is what life should be.

I feel that all aspects of life have their reason and Education is where I always wanted to be, fancies here and their, Fantasies here and there.

My greatest tasks are challenges and so many upsets I have overcome. From extra un-ordinary decisions about life and how to carry on, because someone wasn't going to be their and all along you know where you should have stood. "Life is funny" and that's how I understand family and friends.

I like to have friends and family and try to do my best to get along. Preparing for success is like always a struggle it seems to me, I 'am probably different but still a person. Struggle to me is pulling through, but it's hard to explain. "I need to have good days." But know at the same time I will have bad ones as well.

Thanks to decisions of ones not mine I feel actually in charge of my feelings but still a struggle. Struggling is like art you can wish for better and can do your best to challenge to redeem it. It is better to understand that everything is taken care of. That once you have started something you should always finish it, you may not always be the first person to see it but right along the lines there is still a picture. It takes days and time to free you, but the outcome should have been worth a goal. It probably should have had been worth a desire worth have to have held on to.

To the best of my understanding everything I do seems to always be incomplete, in order to go on another trip worth going to I feel that you have to earn it. Sometimes rather than defying the American dream we understand that "yeah" maybe a little comfort is necessary.

An individual on my behalf always has an idea, and should always confront their every calculated step especially an individual that shows a little concept to what life may be.

Writer's Cramp

Education I do admire, it is almost to me equivalent to the "American dream" being a leader. Being a leader is a sequence to all that unfolds, eras for the meaning of new adults, eras of new technology, and everything else upcoming.

Young and old, wise, wonderers, geniuses, can achieve anything, but it's not by luck it takes respect and self encouragement. Frustrations are probably a novice that probably tends to ignore other frustrations. Frustrating, it also may be that it also knows there are admirations everywhere, and we can all relate to it.

Art and continuing to base art on an everyday account is step by step and not only hard work and dedication but a rhythm of curiosity and is work within the reach and then maybe not so bad after all.

I think that people deny a lot what they started. I really have wanted to explore myself and get open somewhere. I feel that's a good life, not all the time play this and play that. Sometimes that's probably why we can't take life with us, life is always going and sometimes we need it on our side.

Actually I really do not know where I 'am going in life and almost sure of it. I really feel that everyone is leaving, until I 'am around but still then I cant figure out why I'M hurting, really I do my best to get out. Things in life are seemingly easy to me, I always felt like I could do everything though. "My bad, I got into it."

I want to see the outdoors after some kind of career like ordinary people do. I like the outdoors, the nature walks I have done a few.
I feel like the people around me do to, I wonder why the world looks the way it does and what's available.

Writer's Cramp

Nairda's Dimensions

Footnotes

These words in Nairda's Dimensions are exactly as expressed by Adrian.

Paragraphs were added only for emphasis and comprehension.

Adrian is a naturally gifted artist, which is perhaps balance for other Dimensions.

A book entitled "Nairda's Dimensions" will be published by TumbleBrush Press with more of Adrian's writing interspersed with reproductions of his art and reflections about both by a friend.

Adrian's words are Enchanting.

Adrian's art is Inspiring.

Your Spirit will revel in the exposition of
Angel Adrian
when you embrace "Nairda's Dimensions".

Extractions from Humanity

Introducing Cliff

Encountering Cliff is always Delightfully Defining because Cliff discovers himself with each moment of living.

You see, Cliff is enabled with incredible sensitivities not common to most of us.

Cliff feels energy existing everywhere, yet ignored by most of us, because we are too busy bustling with mundane reverberations from silliness required by accumulating stuff and then bragging about the effort we spent doing that. As if to offset our silliness, Cliff translates the impressions he sensitizes, which we ignore, into words as Verse Pleading for Recognition.

Cliff discovers treasures in simple objects we throw away. He appreciates craftsmanship, antiquity, design and sponsoring given by nurturing something as if it were a family member. Because he has no need to accumulate anything for himself, Cliff delightedly shares these treasures with others while seeking no recompense.

Writer's Cramp

Being overly Sensitive is a Blessing which can translate into a Burden when sensitivity becomes overwhelming. Such is the plight Cliff ponders as his awareness creates a Chamber of Meditation that captures his energy and occasionally renders him incapacitated for normal interaction. Cliff retreats to a metamorphosis of contemplation that winds to recession and depression. It is a stage organized only by Cliff as he becomes the actors and directors of his own drama until some incident releases him from this Alteration.

Being an extra-sensory form, Cliff experiences inspiration that is available, but not actuated by most of us. He senses sensitivities, contemplates escaped compassion, laments opportunity gambled and mourns memory not honored.

You will adore Cliff's Persona and Performance. He inspires without complication and cares simply. Cliff is an artist Painting Life with Strokes of Sensitivity.

Extractions from Humanity 1

Dear Dad

The Whispers of a Fallen Star
cannot be heard
where you are.

Though you speak to us in silence,
in vain,
We Love you, Dad,
quite the same.

We find it hard to realize
that you have gone
from our eyes.

We cannot find the Words to say
how much we miss you, every day . . .

We wish there were a telephone –

We'd call you up and say
Dad, please come home.

Writer's Cramp

Extractions from Humanity 2

America (The Clydesdale)

Perhaps America

should abandon

the symbol of

the Eagle

and adapt that of

the Clydesdale

because

that

is what America

truly is.

Writer's Cramp

Extractions from Humanity 3

Dogmatically Stigmatized

Just remember
just because
you Love someone
does not mean
that they
will love you back.

Just because
you look at them
does not mean
that they
are not looking away.

You say one thing
but they think another.

Sometimes
you articulate
with the Heart
and for that
they call you Stupid.

I guess

some things

Writer's Cramp

are simply
not to be
understood.

Especially
born black
with
the mark of
Boy.

A Father
A Grandfather
A Great-uncle
and still
Boy.

It is obvious
even Greens
nor a chunk of meat
remain the same.

It is obvious
that
the human condition
is
an inaccurate
enforce
of Governance.

Whispers 1

From Cliff

About Wisdom

Wisdom

is learning

to deal with

your own

stupidity.

Extracting significance from common experiences is a gift. Cliff is gifted. His perspective formed from his desire to comprehend encounters with humanity, with objects exhibiting energy, and with Spirit. Every connection to a vibration offering inquiry is reason for Cliff to examine. Declarations from those observations are profoundly exhibited in his book, "Extractions From Humanity".

Writer's Cramp

Extractions from Humanity 6

Priceless Value

The Ignorance

of our society

is that

we have yet

to discover

what Value

there is

in not placing

a monetary value

on things

that are Priceless.

Extractions from Humanity 10

Obama Ittis
(Bushwhacked)

If there are not
enough fools
in our society
for us to make
a living by
and increase
our wealth

Then we shall create them.

For it is fools
that are big business.

It matters not
that the over-all economy
goes to Hell.

If it stinks

we shall vote in
a Black President
and blame him
for the fallout.

Extractions from Humanity 33

True Manhood

The price of true Manhood
is greater
than what many
are willing
or capable
of mustering.

To put others first
is
the ultimate virtue

and

is the Epitome of good Fathering.

What good
has a man served
if he
has not reached
these heights?

Extractions from Humanity 34

Acute Humility

The one
who cannot be reached
by Acute Humility
of another

has an issue
that can only
be fixed by GOD.

However,

the one
who is conquered
by Gentle Kindness
of another . . .

I ask –

"What can be
more Humbling
than this?"

Writer's Cramp

Extractions from Humanity 24

InFinite

The True meaning

of InFinite

can be found

in the ultimate

Power

of a Woman.

Extractions from Humanity 65

Question for the Vain

Most people

are

as nutty as a Fruitcake

and don't KNOW it.

I

on the other hand

am as Nutty as Fruitcake

but I KNOW it...

now

is that VANITY??

Honoring Cliff

Transmuting 4

Sharing

treasures

of spirit and matter

discarded

by insensitive forces

rejuvenates and rejoices

intent and invention.

It is the bequest

of Angels.

Cliff is a professional 'scrapper' discovering respect for all things and all people. Cliff's attention and affection transforms 'useless' to 'utility'. His aura gifts value to everything.

Writer's Cramp

Extractions from Humanity 121

A Very Wealthy Man

Today

I Declare

the best day

of my life

for

I start proceeds

to become

a very wealthy man.

I shall gather poop

spitballs and mud,

package them,

market them

Writer's Cramp

and then

sell them

to the DeFence Department

Extractions from Humanity 150

Trina

I wonder
if sweetness
can be
sweet enough
to burn the tongue
of
he who loves her.

Does it matter
that the tune
of
her music
stuns.

That
Great Gladiators
would beg
to be hers.

Her
devastation
kills pain
that she
cooks

Writer's Cramp

like the
Lady of the Knight

and her
soft touch
sooths
anxiety
of the
Hungry Lion.

I wonder
if
the milk
of her spirit
is
so nourishing
that
men
and boys
cry
over drops of it.

Can she talk
without
bringing tears
to the eyes
of
a stranger.

Writer's Cramp

Can she manage
her

daily affairs

without someone

Wanting her.

Does she even
know how
to say yes
to anything
that beckons
for
Her Treasure.

Writer's Cramp

Honoring Spirit

Cliff II
12

When Spirit

throbs

with so many dimensions,

Honoring replicates.

Co-joining Spirit

Eclipses genealogy.

Cliff's spirit permeates space and time. Cliff honors by his presence. Honoring him with abundant messages honors our awareness of spirit profound.

Extractions from Humanity 176

Trials And Tribulations

If

trials

and tribulations

are designed

with the intent

of God

to make us stronger

and build character

Why do we

try to pray them

away?

Writing

By Cliff

The Liberty of Writing

Slowly
"I've Got The Blues"!
And Ever
Saith the Poet
so gradually
and I care not
Comes the Entry
As to who knows
Into the Mind
"And furthermore,
Of a written Work
Any Human, Animal
or species, Alive
And
or Dead, In Limbo
Though it's Pergatory
Molecular Structure
Even those of us
Can only Be Identified
Who Thuss stand
By the Wonder
Before the Thresholds

That moves It
of the After Life
Into the Reality
can kiss my
of Thoughts,
Got Damed A_ _ !!!
Its Words Articulates
Are Put Together
(Never The Less)
Between the Storms
of Heaven and Hell

Extractions from Humanity

A Collection of Observations

Cliff presents us with verse naturally extracted from his Observations conducted during daily encounters with humanity and Spirit.

These are not musings propelled by formal education or classical learning. These are raw realizations erupting with geyser force to declare Sensitivity.

The pages labeled "Extractions" are Cliff's creations. "Whispers" are documentation of Cliff's verbal extractions. "Honoring" are observations from a friend and admirer.

Discover an author who never dreamed of being published. Embrace a translator mining the treasures of Soul. Enjoy a quarry of gems that will become a full presentation as "Extractions From Humanity" by Clifford Ray Garrett.

Determine that you are capable to express your own gifts of Observation.

Extract from your own experiences and then, Express.

Writer's Cramp

Explore Spirit. Mine your Mind.

Gift with one word and then another.

Extract gems with Soul.

Become a Prism.

Write.

The American Dream

An Immigrant's Story

Expressions of culture, family, immigration, frustration, searching, struggling, seeking to belong and finally, resolution of sorts, is common to another generation of America's family. Ivan is an expressive member of these messengers.

Ivan's dreams are literally repeated by millions of Souls seeking comfort, support for family and peacefulness.

Ivan has no training for writing. His natural energy and enthusiasm propelled these expressions and we are blessed to present them as Demonstration of natural composition.

The American Dream

One

I blamed everyone for my problems, for my bad luck, for being chubby... why me, why couldn't I've be born in the next house, with los "camacho" They were like 5 brothers and 2 sisters, they were poor also, but they managed somehow to live just a bit better than us, they always dressed nicer than everyone,

I remember this one time when my neighbor walked down the street and said "look it's a zaga" while pointing at his under wear, "zaga" was a fancy brand like "calvin klein" and to make things worse his name was also ivan, he was skinny and always had kaki pants and dressing shirts that the old brothers had given him, clothes were big on him but we were so ignorant that we said, "men, they always have nice clothes" we used to go to " la segunda" those were the stores where americans would sell their used clothes, the bigger the nike logo or the polo or whatever american brand you fancied the better,

There' is not such thing as a civilized conversation between two young people, they always compete, who's got the better sound system, who's is more expensive, who's shoes are older, I can't tell you how embarrassed I feel when I remember that I used to be like that, nobody gives positive feedback for any accomplishments you made no matter how small,....always making fun of anything you want to try or improve or learn, for example me, I always loved martial arts, bruce lee, van dame, I joined a kick boxing club when I was 13 or 14 I don't remember, but I paid my own monthly membership my rent my food, gave money to my mom, had money for my own shoes and a " can of coke" my family feedback? .....What! Do you think you are bruce lee now?! You are a fat ass! Can barely carry your own gut! Much less jump and kick!

I can't imagine my self telling something like that to anybody, and my family less, I threw a party for my daughter when she was second place on a spelling bee contest! I want her to feel that every single good thing that she does makes me so proud i cry!

Why was so hard to show love and affection in my family, If i were to tell my cousin that I miss him and really value his friendship I would've been called a fag, my own cousin would call me that, " so seas puto wey!" Don't be a fag translated ...I don't hate anybody anymore, I don't blame anybody anymore, I used to tho, ,,,,until I kinda start getting out of it....Ignorance I blame, I don't blame anybody just ignorance

The American Dream

Two

For my luck it wasn't like that, like in the soap operas, they did feed me dinner and let me stay until it got dark, I was kind of looking around imagining where I would sleep in this fancy house, (at least for me it was fancy) then my friends mom came to us and said "well ivan, you see is getting late and we need to go to sleep, you guys can play tomorrow " ok I said waiting for her to tell me where I was supposed to sleep, she looked at me and then at the door, ….oh! Right I said as I walked towards the door …ok…see you tomorrow,

I walked outside, just in the other side of the block where my house was, ….ok…..now what? Should I just go back home? Should I…..damn it! I got nowhere to go! My mom will beat the crap out of me if I go back, my grandpa! Yes that's it my blood, my dads dad, I never really knew Them, they hated my mom, they said she was a slut,

my grandfather was a "player" he had 3 women that he dated while being with my fathers mom, he had 3 more kids with different a woman and 3 with my dads mom, the few times I saw them

They told me crap about my mom and step dad, They were hurt that she didn't mourn my dad for more than a few months, they would always give me money when I saw them, not a lot, just enough for a soda and a bag of chips,

but back then and probably until now still "fancy" to drink a can of coke in the street, some people will even walk around with an empty can just so that other people would've like " wow" that was my only option, my "grandfather family " so I went to my uncles house, all of my dads family were cab drivers and carpenters,

I walked in as I usually did when I was craving a soda and chips, we knew the routine, hey uncle how are You? Hey nephew! How you been? How's life, You hungry?   Blah, blah, blah, …..30 minutes and I was out the door with,   5,10 or even sometimes 20 pesos, …..but not this time….this time I kinda of really needed them, what's the big deal, They were my dads brothers, (at least from same dad) they always pretended to be happy to see me and told me we were family, so I walked in…after the blah blah, I stayed quiet and pretended to be sad, (I wasn't but I need a place to sleep and I needed help)

...what's wrong my uncle asked,.....nothing I nod, ...come on what's the matter? ....I stayed quiet a little longer.....I ran from home

.....what? Why?....after explaining what happened and told them I had enough they said,.... ok, well contact your grand mom, (my moms mom) she always protected and spoiled me once in a while, and I don't know if she did it out of love or just to bother my mom,

in my family and maybe a lot of people do that and that's just the way it is.

The American Dream

Footnotes

Ivan is an immigrant. His Dream was to come to America and prosper.

Ivan is now a father, husband, small business owner and is honoring his extended family with mentoring, valuing and support.

Ivan wrote these passages on his DROID X and transmitted them by e-mail.

Paragraphs were added only for emphasis and comprehension. Otherwise, the writing is exactly as expressed and presented by Ivan.

It's a Gift to receive someone's Heart through their written expressions. Ivan offers us his Spirit and insight without compromise.

Training and editing might 'polish' these words, but that could also diminish their potency.

AngelMagic

Laura-Arual

All of us connect with our surroundings and with each other.

Some Earthly Spirits embrace Awareness resounding communication with Angels.

Laura dwells in AngelRainbows.

To most of us, Angels are mythical imaginations fluttering with escape from our daily traumas, only when we exhaust other remedies to self-inflicted desperation.

For Laura, Angels are the cherubs, children, and cherished connections who are language for Spirit expressing Serene dimensions. Angels are Laura's vocabulary for declaring her sensitivity.

Laura is gifted to express, expose and espouse AngelMagic.

Laura's journey to AngelExpression has been a continual quest to discover comfort with compelling connections that most of us ignore for the glamour of 'things' and 'trinkets' that puff our ego and narcissism while disguising our Spirituality.

Laura is also Arual, who inspires flute players and other musicians of heart-harmonies welding harmonies of Soul.

Discover your own vocabulary of AngelMagic in Laura's Writing Demonstrated.

Construct AngelWords to express
your own connections.

Display AngelRainbows,
Every Precious Moment.

Every Precious Moment

One

There are moments in time that alter realities forever.

I recently experienced one – no, several – of those moments in the last few days. They began with the ring of the telephone. I was working in my room at my Holistic Health Center, doing a massage when I heard fateful words through the door; "She's dead! Slow down, slow down. Tell me what happened."

I ran out the door to the front and found my friend and co-worker, Dr. Kathi, gripping the phone with one hand, covering her mouth with the other in shock, and crying. Her granddaughter, Daxie, had died instantly in an horrendous car accident. Katie, Kathi's daughter, was driving the car and fortunately had only minor physical injuries.

We were out the door within 2 minutes and on the scene within 10 minutes. It was horrible. The car was demolished into a million pieces strewn for 75 yards down the road.

Miraculously, Katie had walked away from a car that was completely demolished. The back of the car beyond the driver's seat was simply gone. The passenger seat was crushed and the engine, what was left of it, was crammed into the firewall, and yet the steering wheel was not pushed into the driver's seat. The only glass left on the vehicle was the glass in the driver's window.

There was not a scratch on the entire driver's door and it opened perfectly. It was if Katie had sat in a protective bubble, not to be harmed.

There were four vehicles involved and every single person walked away except one precious little girl, Daxie, an innocent 2½ year old.

Another driver had seen Daxie seconds before the car careened out-of-control. Daxie had looked at him, a total stranger, smiled and waved.

That was her way. She knew no disharmony or strife. She brought peace and love to everyone with whom she came into contact. She was a perfect example of unconditional love, joy and patience.

The driver said afterwards that she looked so pretty, dressed head to toe in pink.

Every Precious Moment

Two

As we arrived on the scene, we realized we had taken a turn onto an overpass that wasn't where we needed to be. Kathi jumped out of the car, ran down the embankment, as I crossed the bridge and parked the car on the opposite side of the freeway.

As I crossed the bridge, I saw Marty, Kathi's best friend, running across the field. It seemed as if she floated very fast towards the road. I pulled up next to her, jumped out of the car, and we clutched one another, moving toward the freeway.

It was heavy with traffic and for a split second I wondered how we were to cross. I put out my hand and as if I pulled a red light out of my pocket, the front line of those cars simultaneously stopped. I didn't realize the implications of this until later. We walked across the freeway to find Kathi.

The scene was not pleasant. Katie, overwrought with grief and disbelief, was in the ambulance insisting not to be taken anywhere until her mother, Kathi, got there.

As we arrived on the scene, Daxie instantly contacted me. She was swirling above me, asking "What's happening? Why is everyone so unhappy? I'm OK. Why can't Mommy hear me?"

I silently told Daxie that she was dead and no longer in physical form and everyone was very sad that she was gone.

She replied, "But I here" in a two-year old vernacular.

I was standing next to Kathi at that point and she looked at me, recognizing the look on my face and what I was doing and said, "She's here, isn't she?"

Daxie, immediately upon being recognized by her grandmother, said, "Gigi, I'm right here. I'm OK. Don't cry."

Kathi began talking to her, telling her how much we loved her and helped Daxie to feel better about her situation. Daxie knew then that someone was listening besides me.

I was vibrating so intensely, I could hardly stand. The kinetic energy of the situation was intense. The re-routing of traffic created this revolving effect on the energy and with everyone's attention placed on the scene, it was difficult to overcome the massiveness of it

and bring light onto the area.

It had become a great sinkhole of energy. Most of it negative human emotions of fear and anger. It was bigger than big. I did manage to ground myself and felt, after awhile, that I had opened a small portal of light. I had been telepathically calling several of my friends and asking for help and light to clear this area and help me stay focused and upright.

A couple of days later, two of my friends asked me what time all this had taken place because they had very loud ringing in their ears that very afternoon. I said, "That was me calling you. And apparently something in you heard me because I know I had some help. Thanks."

We also found out later that a friend of Kathi was caught up in the traffic and had an almost overwhelming feeling of foreboding when she heard on the radio that it was a fatality accident. She was very upset and didn't know why, until later when she heard who was involved.

Another friend of ours, a few days later, asked me exactly where the accident had taken place, because every day as she drove down that road, she would get goose bumps at a

certain spot. Of course, it was the exact location where it had occurred.

You see, we are all connected, and if we would just remember how to communicate with our ears through our hearts, much more compassion and peace would be at hand.

After what seemed an eternity, what with police reports, paramedics, firemen, onlookers, and hoards of press cameras, we loaded Katie up and took her to the doctor.

Every Precious Moment

Three

Later that evening, close friends and family gathered at Aunt Marty's house. Kathi was making phone calls and contacted some other women who do similar work as she and I do with energy; healing and higher Beings. They offered to come over and assist us in a candle lighting ceremony to honor Daxie and recognize her gifts to each of us. We were very thankful for their support.

After they arrived and the circle was set, Daxie came to me, gave me one of her diminutive looks with a sly little smile on her face and transformed instantly into an incredible light being. She was at least five stories tall and absolutely radiant.

I was somewhat surprised because of the instantaneousness of it. I said I really didn't expect that, and she slowly, miraculously morphed back into the little Daxie I knew and asked me, "Would you rather see me this way?"

I said, "No, that's OK. Please manifest to all your splendor. You are absolutely gorgeous!"

She bowed her head slightly and expanded into that magnificent being again. She then swirled and enveloped the entire room with rainbow colors and created a very safe, sacred space for everyone there.

This puzzled me because of the work I have done with people who have passed over. Most all humans, when they die, spend some time close to beloved ones and then move on to the spirit world to continue their work. If their life has been none too loving, they are sent to a place to release the pain, learn a few lessons before they get to do their work, or come back here.

I have never witnessed anyone instantaneously evolve into their highest form. I was astonished. The purity and innocence of her soul had not been tarnished by fear or hate, or any human belief that keeps most of us from our divinity. She was pure and perfect.

The simple ceremony was beautiful and left us with a sense of peace and some closure. We did our very best to honor Daxie and her short life with us.

When asked what she brought to me, I replied, "conscious innocence."

Every Precious Moment

Four

Daxie never lost Awareness of who she was or where she came from. She lived a life of love, joy and innocence with faith in every person for their goodness and recognized the perfection in every single event and situation.

There are many children among us now, who are very old souls and very enlightened, evolved beings who are coming in now to take humankind into the next evolutionary step of consciousness.

The Indigos, as they are often called, are being born everyday, more and more, and it is up to us to recognize them and honor their journey and their sacrifice. We are here to encourage them and help them to develop ways in which to exist on this planet right now.

Someone said that Daxie was a great Angel who came to visit us for awhile and teach us how to live and love, and that she would be back.

Beings of this nature cannot exist in density of negative emotions. The hate and fear that envelopes our world today is simply too dense and dirty for them to stay in a form that most humans can actually see. They must take on so much density to be seen that they take on too much negativity at the same time and cannot maintain that form for very long.

It takes tremendous amounts of energy to hold density for human eyes to see. And, the reality is that most humans become startled or frightened if they do see something out-of-the-ordinary, or simply dismiss their visions immediately.

Daxie came from another time and place. She dropped in to see what condition our condition was in. She did all she could for as long as she could, and then left.

She was definitely aware that she was leaving. She gave many messages in her own innocent way, that in hindsight, are profound for us as we reminisce about her last few hours with us.

A few days before Daxie left, she picked up a book at her Gigi's (Kathi) house, authored by Mike Van Praugh, entitled, "Talking to Heaven". She handed to her Gigi and said, "Here Gigi, I read this."

I told Kathi that was Daxie's way of saying, "Here, I'm leaving. Call me."

Every Precious Moment

Footnotes

As the typist who typed "Every Precious Moment" from hardcopy

into computer format,

attempted to type grandmother Kathi's name into the text,

the actual letters that initially appeared, were

Dathi.

AngelMagic

Diary of an Angel

This diary was written by a very special little Angel passed to AngelSpace. Her name is Daxie.

Dear Diary:
I had so much fun today playing with my friends here in the Valley. I'm so excited. Muriel, our caretaker, told me it would be soon that I could go to Earth and be a little girl for awhile. My friends and I have been waiting to go for a long time. Muriel takes care of us every day. She teaches us how to live in harmony and peace. We made friends with all the birds and animals. Bobby Peacock is my favorite because he is so beautiful.

Muriel says this Valley is a very special place. It's where Angels like my friends and I live and play before we get to be born as little boys and girls. Muriel says we have to stay here until our mommies and daddies are ready for us on Earth.

Stephen, Micah, Michael, Gabrielle, Serrah, Max and I have wanted to go for a long time. But, Muriel said that when the time is right, we could decide whom we wanted as parents and then we get to go to Earth. It looks like so much fun there. Oh, it's fun here, but I would really like to have a special mommy and daddy just for me.

Today, Muriel told me to pick a mommy so that I could go be her little girl. I have to choose carefully. Muriel told me I am a very loving Angel and that I would be most happy with parents who love me and want a special little girl. So, I have to pick my family very carefully and make sure I will be surrounded by people who recognize who I am and help me not to forget my AngelMagic. Muriel said I could never forget, so that I can come back to this beautiful Valley.

Muriel said that all people are born with AngelMagic but most forget all these things when they grow up. I think that is sad that people forget and I agreed to come back soon. I like talking to all the animals and trees and making leaves dance in my hands. I really love it here with Muriel and all my friends. I'm sure my mommy and daddy will understand when I need to come back, and it will be OK with them.

Muriel told me I have to go to Earth to become a pretty little girl and show every single person how we love one another here in the Valley. She says people are looking for that love and there are many little Angels like me who are being born to show all grownups how to see things the way we do here and how to love one another.

AngelMagic

Healing Hands

Micah had waited for months for his baby sister to come. He was so excited when his mommy said his baby sister would be born in a few days.

She said, "Micah, we're going to name her Hannah and you must be very gentle with her when she arrives. She is only a baby and we must take very good care of her."

Micah knew how to be gentle. He had taken very good care of his kitten when it was just born and he intended to take care of Hannah even better.

The next day, Micah went to sleepover with Aunt Sherrie and his cousin Jason. The following morning when Micah came home, Hannah was there wrapped up in a beautiful pink blanket with angels all over it. She was so pretty. He tiptoed over to her and gently rubbed her arms and kissed her forehead.

He smiled up at his mommy, "I'll take care of her; don't you worry. Nobody will hurt my Hannah."

Writer's Cramp

Micah's mommy smiled and ruffled his hair and said, "I know you'll be a wonderful big brother. Now run along and play. She is sleeping now. I'll call you when she wakes up."

The next several days were very busy. Micah helped mommy with Hannah as much as he could. In the mornings, he helped bathe her. His favorite part was rubbing her with baby lotion after her bath. Hannah seemed to like this very much and Micah knew it made her feel better because it always made him feel good when mommy rubbed his back and legs.

Micah would fetch Hannah's diapers for mommy and make sure Hannah was covered with her angel blanket when she slept. The Angels reminded him of his Angel friend, Daxie. He would have to remember to tell Hannah about Daxie as soon as she could understand.

Daxie had been around Micah for as long as he could remember. Daxie reminded him of Olga the Bear and RainbowLove and helped him to be really good at MindPictures. He couldn't wait to show Hannah all these things.

Hannah was already good at MindPictures, especially if you pictured bright colors. She always laughed when Micah did rainbow color

MindPictures for her and put his forehead on hers. He knew she could see RainbowLove around people because he could, even before he could talk.

One day, Hannah started getting fussy. She whimpered and cried all morning.

Mommy said to Micah, "I think we need to take Hannah to the doctor. I don't know what is wrong with her or why she is crying."

Micah looked at Hannah and noticed her RainbowColors were not very bright around her stomach. He sat down next to her and put his hands gently on her tummy.

"It's OK Hannah. Just stop crying and feel the RainbowColors on your tummy."

Hannah stopped crying and soon went to sleep.

Micah's mommy was very curious about this. She decided not to take Hannah to the doctor because Hannah appeared to be OK and sleeping very peacefully. It was soon forgotten and she didn't ask Micah about anything.

Several days later, Micah was in his room waiting to go to the park. Mommy had said that they would go to the park after lunch. He went to find her. She was lying on the couch and

didn't look like she felt good. Micah could see her RainbowColors around her head were dark and not bright like they usually were.

"Mommy, what wrong? Don't you feel good?" he asked.

"No, Micah, I've got a very bad headache. We can't go to the park just now. Be a good boy and look in on Hannah and play quietly in your room for me."

Micah was disappointed. Mommy had promised they would go to the park to play and now she didn't want to go. He looked in on Hannah. She was taking a nap, so he went to his room to play. He didn't want to play in his room and he was getting angry and started to kick his toys around when Daxie, his Angel friend, showed up.

"Micah, why are you being so angry? It's not helping anything that you kick your toys."

Micah replied defiantly, "I want to go to the park! Mommy has a stupid headache and now she doesn't want to go."

Daxie perched on top of his dresser.

"Micah, don't you remember how to help your mommy with her headache?"

He paused, "Can I use my RainbowColors on her to help her head?"

"Yes, Micah. And you can use your RainbowStones to help too."

Micah grinned, grabbed has bag of stones and ran to the couch where his mommy lay.

"Mommy, mommy, let me help with your headache!"

She just smiled.

Micah looked at mommy's RainbowColors and saw that the colors around her head were not very bright. He walked over to her, and pulled out two stones from his bag that would help make those colors bright again. He then placed them on her forehead and put his hands on the sides of her head and sat down next to her on the couch.

Micah leaned over mommy and whispered, "Look at the RainbowColors inside your head and feel my colors around you."

The frown on her face began to relax. She looked up at him and smiled.

"You're a special little boy, Micah. I don't know what you are doing, but you've got a MagicTouch. My headache is going away. Thank you so much. Some day I want you to teach mommy how to do this."

"Mommy, you already can. Just remember how to do your AngelMagic."

She smiled. "Micah, I don't know what you're talking about, but maybe I can remember if you will help me."

"OK," he said. "Just close your eyes and picture RainbowColors coming out of your hands. It feels warm when you touch someone. Here, put your hands on my back. Just imagine this white light coming our of your hands and into my back. Yeah, just like that. Now picture different colors coming out. That's great, mommy. I can feel that. Can't you?"

"Well, Micah, I'm not sure. Maybe I need some practice."

"Sure, the more you do it, the stronger it gets. Try it on Hannah next time she gets fussy."

Mommy ruffled his hair. "I'll do that and thanks for helping with my headache."

Micah skipped off to play with his baby sister; forgetting about the park.

Later that day when daddy got home, he said he had a rough day. He sat down heavily in his favorite chair.

Micah bounced in and jumped on his lap. "Daddy, will you play catch with me?"

"Oh, Micah, let me sit here and rest. I've had a very tiring day, so maybe we'll play later."

Micah saw that it was getting late and knew that his daddy would not want to play much later. He went to the kitchen where mommy was cooking and sat heavily in his own chair.

"What's wrong little man?" mommy asked.

Micah sighed, "Daddy's tired and doesn't feel like playing with me."

Mommy winked, "Well maybe I can use my AngelMagic on him and he'll feel better to play with you."

Micah beamed. Mommy went to daddy and put her hands on his head and then his heart and

rubbed his back for a few minutes. Micah could see daddy's RainbowColors come alive.

Writer's Cramp

Mommy bent down to daddy's ear and whispered, "Maybe you feel good enough now to play with Micah before dinner."

Daddy shrugged his shoulders, stretched and said, "I don't know what you did, but I feel lots of energy now."

Looking at Micah, he said, "Let's go Sport!"

Micah smiled at mommy and she winked back.

That night just as Micah was about to fall asleep in his bed, Daxie appeared.

"Quite a day, huh Micah?"

"It was great, Daxie. I helped mommy remember her AngelMagic and my RainbowStones really work. I want to get Hannah her own stones."

"Micah, those will come along in time. Let Hannah pick her own. She will know exactly what she needs in her MedicineBag when the time comes. Right now, you just keep remembering your AngelMagic and help other

to remember theirs'. You're a special little boy. Sweet dreams and good night."

Daxie showered Micah with AngelDust and went to find other boys and girls who were remembering their AngelMagic.

AngelMagic

AngelNotes

Laura DeMatteis is responsible for conveying the messages and magic in AngelMagic.

Except for cosmetic changes, the words and AngelDust you experience are blessedly transferred to us by Laura's sensitivity, Awareness and communication with Angels.

AngelMagic is available to all of us. Awareness is the only ingredient separating us from this Serenity.

You might construe that Laura's gift to communicate and express these miracles is a special endowment. But, Laura prays you to understand that this is available to anyone who chooses to participate.

A book titled "AngelMagic" will be presented with other AngelWords translated by Laura.

Compile your own dictionary of AngelExpressions.

Dwell with AngelRainbows.

Writer's Cramp

Choose RainbowStones.

Discover Angels.

Be an Angel.

Writer's Cramp

Writer's Cramp

The Spirita Collection

A Book of Dibbles

Blossoms n' Bubbles

Conversations with Grasshopper

Inspirations – Honoring Soul

Rainbows for Marina

Snippettes of Spirit

SymPhonetic Musings

The Flute Player of Sasnak

available at:

www.TumblebrushPress.com

Share your own inspirations with us:
inspirations@tumblebrushpress.com

Writer's Cramp

www.ingramcontent.com/pod-product-compliance
Lightning Source LLC
Chambersburg PA
CBHW060824050426
42453CB00008B/584